Family Keepsake Journal

Dad, I WANT TO Learn Your Recipes

A KEEPSAKE MEMORY BOOK TO GATHER AND PRESERVE YOUR FAVORITE FAMILY RECIPES

Jeffrey Mason

This journal contains the recipes of

_____

INTRODUCTION

Family recipes are much more than written down instructions on how to cook things. They are connection and they are memories.

Cooking from a recipe written in your in your father's handwriting carries you to his side, chopping and stirring in unison. Cooking a dish the way he taught you fills each chop, stir, and step with the magic of memories.

A recipe can pull a child, who has since grown and moved away, back to a long-ago afternoon cooking with their dad. A recipe can seat us at the memory of a crowded table packed full of family, celebrating holidays, and stoking traditions that have lived on through decades past.

That is the magic of food. Eating involves and includes all of our senses, creating the perfect bond to hold our memories close. Add to that the feelings and emotions of being with the people we love, and the simplest dish or the most weathered recipe card can entangle itself with who and how we are.

That is the purpose of this book.

Dad, I Want to Learn Your Recipes preserves and continues the legacy of your family's traditions. It creates a record of what has been eaten and enjoyed and provides a way to hand it on and on and on.

HOW TO USE THIS BOOK

If You are Giving This Book to Someone Else

If this book is being given as a gift, the next two pages provide a place for you to write down the recipes you would like to be shared with you.

There is space for fifty recipes. Please don't worry if you can't think of that many. The extra spaces provide room for your dad to add dishes he thinks should be detailed and kept.

Be sure to include recipes you personally enjoy, as well as those that are linked to family traditions.

Each recipe includes prompts and space to encourage the recipient to share the story and memories of each one.

If You Have Been Given This Book or Bought it For Yourself

If the next two pages have the names of the recipes you are being asked to share, you can use that as a guide. If not, feel free to share the recipes you feel should be recorded and passed on.

Each recipe is followed by a series of questions, encouraging you to write about any associated stories and memories. There is also space to share your memories of cooking, food, and the many traditions that they are often a part of.

Dad, When I Think Back, These are the Recipes I Would Love for you to Share

1. _____
2. _____
3. _____
4. _____
5. _____
6. _____
7. _____
8. _____
9. _____
10. _____
11. _____
12. _____

> "FATHERS ARE MEN WHO DARED TO PLACE THE WORLD'S HOPES AND DREAMS IN THEIR CHILDREN."

— Author Unknown

RECIPE TABLE OF CONTENTS

Recipe 1 : _____ 10

Recipe 2 : _____ 14

Recipe 3 : _____ 18

Recipe 4 : _____ 22

Recipe 5 : _____ 26

Recipe 6 : _____ 32

Recipe 7 : _____ 36

Recipe 8 : _____ 40

Recipe 9 : _____ 44

Recipe 10 : _____ 50

Recipe 11 : _____ 54

Recipe 12 : _____ 58

Recipe 13 : _____ 62

Recipe 14 : _____ 66

Recipe 15 : _____ 70

Recipe 16 : _____ 76

Recipe 17 : _____ 80

Recipe 18 : _____ 84

Recipe 19 : _____ 88

Recipe 20 : _____ 92

Recipe 21 : _____	98
Recipe 22 : _____	102
Recipe 23 : _____	106
Recipe 24 : _____	110
Recipe 25 : _____	114
Recipe 26 : _____	120
Recipe 27 : _____	124
Recipe 28 : _____	128
Recipe 29 : _____	132
Recipe 30 : _____	136
Recipe 31 : _____	142
Recipe 32 : _____	146
Recipe 33 : _____	150
Recipe 34 : _____	154
Recipe 35 : _____	158
Recipe 36 : _____	164
Recipe 37 : _____	168
Recipe 38 : _____	172
Recipe 39 : _____	176
Recipe 40 : _____	180
Recipe 41 : _____	186
Recipe 42 : _____	190

Recipe 43 : _____ 194

Recipe 44 : _____ 198

Recipe 45 : _____ 202

Recipe 46 : _____ 208

Recipe 47 : _____ 212

Recipe 48 : _____ 216

Recipe 49 : _____ 220

Recipe 50 : _____ 224

"A RECIPE IS A STORY THAT ENDS WITH A GOOD MEAL."

– PAT CONROY

Recipe 1 : _____

Serves : _____ **Prep Time :** _____ **Cook Time :** _____

INGREDIENTS :

INSTRUCTIONS :

Hear Your Story Family Keepsake Recipe Journal

Where did you learn this recipe?

THE STORY OF THIS RECIPE

The story of how I learned this recipe is... _____
_____
_____
_____
_____

This is how long it has been in the family... _____
_____
_____

The last time I cooked it was... _____
_____
_____

This is how I would describe how it should taste... _____
_____
_____

And this is the way it makes the house smell when it is cooking... _____
_____
_____

When I think back and remember eating this, these are the memories that come to mind...

_____
_____
_____
_____

MY FOOD STORY IS...

The food or dish that I most associate with growing up is... _____
_____
_____

The person who usually made it was... _____
_____

A specific memory this dish creates for me is... _____
_____
_____
_____
_____

Recipe 2 : _____

Serves : _____ **Prep Time :** _____ **Cook Time :** _____

INGREDIENTS:

- _____
- _____
- _____
- _____
- _____
- _____
- _____
- _____
- _____

- _____
- _____
- _____
- _____
- _____
- _____
- _____
- _____
- _____

INSTRUCTIONS :

_____
_____
_____

Where did you learn this recipe?

THE STORY OF THIS RECIPE

The story of how I learned this recipe is... _____
_____
_____
_____
_____

This is how long it has been in the family... _____
_____
_____

The last time I cooked it was... _____
_____
_____

This is how I would describe how it should taste... _____
_____
_____

And this is the way it makes the house smell when it is cooking... _____
_____
_____

When I think back and remember eating this, these are the memories that come to mind...

_____
_____
_____
_____

MY FOOD STORY IS...

This is who did most of the cooking when I was growing up..._____
_____
_____
_____
_____

Their biggest influence on the way I cook is... _____
_____
_____
_____
_____
_____
_____

Recipe 3 : _____

Serves : _____ **Prep Time :** _____ **Cook Time :** _____

INGREDIENTS :

- _____
- _____
- _____
- _____
- _____
- _____
- _____
- _____
- _____

- _____
- _____
- _____
- _____
- _____
- _____
- _____
- _____
- _____

INSTRUCTIONS :

_____

_____

_____

Hear Your Story Family Keepsake Recipe Journal

Where did you learn this recipe?

THE STORY OF THIS RECIPE

The story of how I learned this recipe is... _____

_____

_____

_____

_____

This is how long it has been in the family... _____

_____

_____

The last time I cooked it was... _____

_____

_____

This is how I would describe how it should taste... _____

_____

_____

And this is the way it makes the house smell when it is cooking... _____

_____

_____

When I think back and remember eating this, these are the memories that come to mind...

_____
_____
_____
_____

MY FOOD STORY IS...

When I was growing up, we typically ate dinner together as a family this many times each week...
_____

When we did eat together, the meal would follow this routine... _____
_____
_____
_____

During these dinners, we usually talked about... _____
_____
_____
_____

Recipe 4 : _____

Serves : _____ **Prep Time :** _____ **Cook Time :** _____

INGREDIENTS :

- _____
- _____
- _____
- _____
- _____
- _____
- _____
- _____
- _____

- _____
- _____
- _____
- _____
- _____
- _____
- _____
- _____
- _____

INSTRUCTIONS :

_____

_____

_____

Hear Your Story Family Keepsake Recipe Journal

Where did you learn this recipe?

THE STORY OF THIS RECIPE

The story of how I learned this recipe is... _____
_____
_____
_____
_____

This is how long it has been in the family... _____
_____
_____

The last time I cooked it was... _____
_____
_____

This is how I would describe how it should taste... _____
_____
_____

And this is the way it makes the house smell when it is cooking... _____
_____
_____

When I think back and remember eating this, these are the memories that come to mind...

_____
_____
_____
_____

MY FOOD STORY IS...

When I was a kid, the favorite dish my parents prepared was... _____
_____
_____

When I think back and remember eating this, these are the memories that come to mind... _____
_____
_____
_____

This is how my version of this dish compares to theirs... _____
_____
_____
_____

Recipe 5 : _____

Serves : _____ **Prep Time :** _____ **Cook Time :** _____

INGREDIENTS :

INSTRUCTIONS :

Where did you learn this recipe?

THE STORY OF THIS RECIPE

The story of how I learned this recipe is... _____
_____
_____
_____
_____

This is how long it has been in the family... _____
_____
_____

The last time I cooked it was... _____
_____
_____

This is how I would describe how it should taste... _____
_____
_____

And this is the way it makes the house smell when it is cooking... ___
_____
_____

When I think back and remember eating this, these are the memories that come to mind...

_____
_____
_____
_____

MY FOOD STORY IS...

When I was a kid, my favorite dish that my grondparents prepared was... _____
_____
_____

When I think back and remember eating this item, these are the memories that come to mind... ___
_____
_____
_____

This is how my version of this dish compares to theirs... _____
_____
_____
_____

"A FATHER CARRIES PICTURES WHERE HIS MONEY USED TO BE."

– STEVEN MARTIN

MY FOOD STORY IS...

When I was growing up, the person who was the best cook in the whole family was... _____
_____
_____
_____
_____

When I think of them, these are a few of the foods, recipes, and dishes that come to mind... _____
_____
_____
_____
_____
_____
_____
_____
_____
_____
_____

Recipe 6 : _____

Serves : _____ **Prep Time :** _____ **Cook Time :** _____

INGREDIENTS :

INSTRUCTIONS :

Hear Your Story Family Keepsake Recipe Journal

Where did you learn this recipe?

THE STORY OF THIS RECIPE

The story of how I learned this recipe is… _____
_____
_____
_____
_____

This is how long it has been in the family… _____
_____
_____

The last time I cooked it was… _____
_____
_____

This is how I would describe how it should taste… _____
_____
_____

And this is the way it makes the house smell when it is cooking… _____
_____
_____

When I think back and remember eating this, these are the memories that come to mind...

_____
_____
_____
_____

MY FOOD STORY IS...

A favorite food or cooking related memory for my childhood is... _____

Recipe 7 : _____

Serves : _____ **Prep Time :** _____ **Cook Time :** _____

INGREDIENTS :

INSTRUCTIONS :

Where did you learn this recipe?

THE STORY OF THIS RECIPE

The story of how I learned this recipe is… _____
_____
_____
_____
_____

This is how long it has been in the family… _____
_____
_____

The last time I cooked it was… _____
_____
_____

This is how I would describe how it should taste… _____
_____
_____

And this is the way it makes the house smell when it is cooking… _____
_____
_____

When I think back and remember eating this, these are the memories that come to mind...

_____
_____
_____
_____

MY FOOD STORY IS...

A home's kitchen and dining area is often the emotional center and gathering place of the family — the heart of the home. When I reflect back on the kitchen I most remember from my childhood, these are the details I remember and the feelings I get... _____

_____
_____
_____
_____
_____
_____
_____
_____
_____

Recipe 8 : _____

Serves : _____ **Prep Time :** _____ **Cook Time :** _____

INGREDIENTS :

INSTRUCTIONS :

Hear Your Story Family Keepsake Recipe Journal

Where did you learn this recipe?

THE STORY OF THIS RECIPE

The story of how I learned to cook this recipe is… _____

_____

_____

_____

_____

This is how long it has been in the family… _____

_____

_____

The last time I cooked it was… _____

_____

_____

This is how I would describe how it should taste… _____

_____

_____

And this is the way it makes the house smell when it is cooking… _____

_____

_____

When I think back and remember eating this, these are the memories that come to mind...

_____
_____
_____
_____

MY FOOD STORY IS...

When I think back to our kitchen growing up, these are the sounds and smells I can still remember when food was being cooked or eaten... _____

_____
_____
_____
_____
_____
_____
_____
_____
_____
_____
_____

Recipe 9 : _____

Serves : _____ **Prep Time :** _____ **Cook Time :** _____

INGREDIENTS :

_____
_____
_____
_____
_____
_____
_____
_____
_____

_____
_____
_____
_____
_____
_____
_____
_____
_____

INSTRUCTIONS :

_____
_____
_____

Hear Your Story Family Keepsake Recipe Journal

Where did you learn this recipe?

THE STORY OF THIS RECIPE

The story of how I learned to cook this recipe is... _____
_____
_____
_____
_____

This is how long it has been in the family... _____
_____
_____

The last time I cooked it was... _____
_____
_____

This is how I would describe how it should taste... _____
_____
_____

And this is the way it makes the house smell when it is cooking... _____
_____
_____

When I think back and remember eating this, these are the memories that come to mind…

_____

_____

_____

_____

MY FOOD STORY IS…

Everyone has a dish or dessert that is THEIR favorite. When I think about my own family growing up, these are the foods I most associate with each of them as being their favorites…

My Mother : _____

My Father : _____

My Siblings : _____

_____

_____

_____

_____

Recipe 10 : _____

Serves : _____ **Prep Time :** _____ **Cook Time :** _____

INGREDIENTS :

INSTRUCTIONS :

Hear Your Story Family Keepsake Recipe Journal

Where did you learn this recipe?

THE STORY OF THIS RECIPE

The story of how I learned to cook this recipe is... _____
_____
_____
_____
_____

This is how long it has been in the family... _____
_____
_____

The last time I cooked it was... _____
_____
_____

This is how I would describe how it should taste... _____
_____
_____

And this is the way it makes the house smell when it is cooking... ___
_____
_____

When I think back and remember eating this, these are the memories that come to mind…

_____
_____
_____
_____

MY FOOD STORY IS…

Family food traditions often come from our ancestors, regional tastes, and our cultural backgrounds and religious practices. The things our family ate that reflected these influences include… _____

_____
_____
_____
_____
_____
_____
_____
_____
_____
_____

"THERE ARE TWO RULES IN BARBEQUE: THE FIRST IS: 'DAD IS IN CHARGE.' THE SECOND IS: 'SEE RULE 1.'"

– AUTHOR UNKNOWN

MY FOOD STORY IS...

When I was growing up, the holiday that was the biggest family event was... _____
_____

The individual(s) who usually prepared the meal on this day was/were... _____
_____
_____

The significant food traditions that were a part of our celebration were... _____
_____
_____
_____
_____
_____
_____
_____
_____
_____

Recipe 11 : _____

Serves : _____ **Prep Time :** _____ **Cook Time :** _____

INGREDIENTS :

- _____
- _____
- _____
- _____
- _____
- _____
- _____
- _____
- _____

- _____
- _____
- _____
- _____
- _____
- _____
- _____
- _____
- _____

INSTRUCTIONS :

_____
_____
_____

Hear Your Story Family Keepsake Recipe Journal

Where did you learn this recipe?

THE STORY OF THIS RECIPE

The story of how I learned to cook this recipe is... _____

_____

_____

_____

_____

This is how long it has been in the family... _____

_____

_____

The last time I cooked it was... _____

_____

_____

This is how I would describe how it should taste... _____

_____

_____

And this is the way it makes the house smell when it is cooking... _____

_____

_____

When I think back and remember eating this, these are the memories that come to mind...

_____
_____
_____
_____

MY FOOD STORY IS...

My favorite holiday has always been... _____
_____
_____

When I reminisce about how we have celebrated this holidat and the traditions that are a part of it, this is what I remember about how that day would ususally go, who we celebrated with, the food we ate, the dishes we used, and the music that was played... _____

_____
_____
_____
_____
_____
_____

Recipe 12 : _____

Serves : _____ **Prep Time :** _____ **Cook Time :** _____

INGREDIENTS :

- _____
- _____
- _____
- _____
- _____
- _____
- _____
- _____
- _____

- _____
- _____
- _____
- _____
- _____
- _____
- _____
- _____
- _____
- _____

INSTRUCTIONS :

_____
_____
_____

Hear Your Story Family Keepsake Recipe Journal

Where did you learn this recipe?

THE STORY OF THIS RECIPE

The story of how I learned to cook this recipe is... _____
_____
_____
_____
_____

This is how long it has been in the family... _____
_____
_____

The last time I cooked it was... _____
_____
_____

This is how I would describe how it should taste... _____
_____
_____

And this is the way it makes the house smell when it is cooking... _____
_____
_____

When I think back and remember eating this, these are the memories that come to mind...

_____
_____
_____
_____

MY FOOD STORY IS...

Of the foods we traditionally had at the holidays and celebrations when I was growing up, the ones that have carried over into the traditions of my adulthood and the family I raised are..._____

_____
_____
_____
_____
_____
_____
_____
_____
_____
_____

Recipe 13 : _____

Serves : _____ **Prep Time :** _____ **Cook Time :** _____

INGREDIENTS :

INSTRUCTIONS :

Hear Your Story Family Keepsake Recipe Journal

Where did you learn this recipe?

THE STORY OF THIS RECIPE

The story of how I learned to cook this recipe is... _____
_____
_____
_____
_____

This is how long it has been in the family... _____
_____
_____

The last time I cooked it was... _____
_____
_____

This is how I would describe how it should taste... _____
_____
_____

And this is the way it makes the house smell when it is cooking... _____
_____
_____

When I think back and remember eating this, these are the memories that come to mind...

_____
_____
_____
_____

MY FOOD STORY IS...

My favorite holiday treat when I was a kid was... _____
_____
_____

My favorite holiday treat now is... _____
_____
_____

For me, the one holiday dish that absolutely has to be served on that day is... _____
_____
_____
_____

Recipe 14 : _____

Serves : _____ **Prep Time :** _____ **Cook Time :** _____

INGREDIENTS :

- _____
- _____
- _____
- _____
- _____
- _____
- _____
- _____
- _____

- _____
- _____
- _____
- _____
- _____
- _____
- _____
- _____
- _____

INSTRUCTIONS :

_____
_____
_____

Hear Your Story Family Keepsake Recipe Journal

Where did you learn this recipe?

THE STORY OF THIS RECIPE

The story of how I learned to cook this recipe is... _____
_____
_____
_____
_____

This is how long it has been in the family... _____
_____
_____

The last time I cooked it was... _____
_____
_____

This is how I would describe how it should taste... _____
_____
_____

And this is the way it makes the house smell when it is cooking... _____
_____
_____

When I think back and remember eating this, these are the memories that come to mind...

_____
_____
_____
_____

MY FOOD STORY IS...

The thing we eat at the holidays that I think we should have more often during the year is... _____
_____
_____

My least favorite holiday side dish is... _____
_____
_____
_____

My favorite holiday leftover is... _____
_____
_____
_____

Recipe 15 : _____

Serves : _____ **Prep Time :** _____ **Cook Time :** _____

INGREDIENTS :

- _____
- _____
- _____
- _____
- _____
- _____
- _____
- _____
- _____

- _____
- _____
- _____
- _____
- _____
- _____
- _____
- _____
- _____

INSTRUCTIONS :

_____
_____
_____

Hear Your Story Family Keepsake Recipe Journal

Where did you learn this recipe?

THE STORY OF THIS RECIPE

The story of how I learned to cook this recipe is... _____
_____
_____
_____
_____

This is how long it has been in the family... _____
_____
_____

The last time I cooked it was... _____
_____
_____

This is how I would describe how it should taste... _____
_____
_____

And this is the way it makes the house smell when it is cooking... _____
_____
_____

When I think back and remember eating this, these are the memories that come to mind...

_____
_____
_____
_____

MY FOOD STORY IS...

If I were to create the perfect holiday menu, it would include the following... _____
_____
_____
_____
_____
_____
_____
_____
_____
_____
_____
_____

"THE OLDER
I GET,
THE SMARTER
MY FATHER
SEEMS TO GET."

— TIM RUSSERT

MY FOOD STORY IS...

When I think back on all of the years we as a family celebrated our favorite holidays, a specific favorite memory I have is...

Recipe 16 : _____

Serves : _____ **Prep Time :** _____ **Cook Time :** _____

INGREDIENTS :

- _____
- _____
- _____
- _____
- _____
- _____
- _____
- _____
- _____

- _____
- _____
- _____
- _____
- _____
- _____
- _____
- _____
- _____

INSTRUCTIONS :

_____
_____
_____

Hear Your Story Family Keepsake Recipe Journal

Where did you learn this recipe?

THE STORY OF THIS RECIPE

The story of how I learned to cook this recipe is... _____

_____

_____

_____

_____

This is how long it has been in the family... _____

_____

_____

_____

The last time I cooked it was... _____

_____

_____

_____

This is how I would describe how it should taste... _____

_____

_____

_____

And this is the way it makes the house smell when it is cooking... _____

_____

_____

When I think back and remember eating this, these are the memories that come to mind…

_____
_____
_____
_____

MY FOOD STORY IS…

In addition to celebrating holidays, food also plays a huge part in our life milestones. An example of this: weddings. For my wedding we served…_____

_____
_____
_____
_____

And we can't forget the cake! At our wedding, this is what ours looked and tasted like…… _____

_____
_____
_____
_____
_____

Recipe 17 : _____

Serves : _____ **Prep Time :** _____ **Cook Time :** _____

INGREDIENTS :

Hear Your Story Family Keepsake Recipe Journal

Where did you learn this recipe?

THE STORY OF THIS RECIPE

The story of how I learned to cook this recipe is… _____
_____
_____
_____
_____

This is how long it has been in the family… _____
_____
_____

The last time I cooked it was… _____
_____
_____

This is how I would describe how it should taste… _____
_____
_____

And this is the way it makes the house smell when it is cooking… _____
_____
_____

When I think back and remember eating this, these are the memories that come to mind...

___

MY FOOD STORY IS...

This is what I love about food and cooking...

Recipe 18 : _____

Serves : _____ **Prep Time :** _____ **Cook Time :** _____

INGREDIENTS :

INSTRUCTIONS :

Hear Your Story Family Keepsake Recipe Journal

Where did you learn this recipe?

THE STORY OF THIS RECIPE

The story of how I learned to cook this recipe is… _____
_____
_____
_____
_____

This is how long it has been in the family… _____
_____
_____

The last time I cooked it was… _____
_____
_____

This is how I would describe how it should taste… _____
_____
_____

And this is the way it makes the house smell when it is cooking… _____
_____
_____

When I think back and remember eating this, these are the memories that come to mind...

_____
_____
_____
_____

MY FOOD STORY IS...

The first thing I learned to cook was... _____
_____
_____

The person who taught me to cook was... _____
_____

When I think about learning to cook this dish, these are the memories that come to mind... _____
_____
_____
_____
_____
_____

Recipe 19 : _____

Serves : _____ **Prep Time :** _____ **Cook Time :** _____

INGREDIENTS :

INSTRUCTIONS :

Where did you learn this recipe?

THE STORY OF THIS RECIPE

The story of how I learned to cook this recipe is... _____
_____
_____
_____
_____

This is how long it has been in the family... _____
_____
_____

The last time I cooked it was... _____
_____
_____

This is how I would describe how it should taste... _____
_____
_____

And this is the way it makes the house smell when it is cooking... _____
_____
_____

When I think back and remember eating this, these are the memories that come to mind...

___

MY FOOD STORY IS...

The way I would describe myself as a cook in my 20's is... ___

A few of my favorite things I most often cooked back then were... ___

Recipe 20 : _____

Serves : _____ **Prep Time :** _____ **Cook Time :** _____

INGREDIENTS :

INSTRUCTIONS :

Hear Your Story Family Keepsake Recipe Journal

Where did you learn this recipe?

THE STORY OF THIS RECIPE

The story of how I learned to cook this recipe is... _____
_____
_____
_____
_____

This is how long it has been in the family... _____
_____
_____
_____

The last time I cooked it was... _____
_____
_____
_____

This is how I would describe how it should taste... _____
_____
_____
_____

And this is the way it makes the house smell when it is cooking... ___
_____
_____
_____

When I think back and remember eating this, these are the memories that come to mind…

___

MY FOOD STORY IS…

Getting married results in the combining of the food preferences and traditions of two individuals and their families. A few of the recipes, dishes, or cooking styles that I discovered from getting married include… ___

"THE COOKBOOKS I VALUE THE MOST ARE THE ONES WHERE YOU HEAR THE AUTHOR'S VOICE IN EVERY RECIPE."

– ANTHONY BOURDAIN

MY FOOD STORY IS...

If I were to create the perfect menu to celebrate an important event in my life, it would include the following... _____

Recipe 21 : _____

Serves : _____ **Prep Time :** _____ **Cook Time :** _____

INGREDIENTS :

INSTRUCTIONS :

Hear Your Story Family Keepsake Recipe Journal

Where did you learn this recipe?

THE STORY OF THIS RECIPE

The story of how I learned to cook this recipe is... _____
_____
_____
_____
_____

This is how long it has been in the family... _____
_____
_____

The last time I cooked it was... _____
_____
_____

This is how I would describe how it should taste... _____
_____
_____

And this is the way it makes the house smell when it is cooking... _____
_____
_____

When I think back and remember eating this, these are the memories that come to mind...

_____
_____
_____
_____

MY FOOD STORY IS...

The way I would describe myself as a cook in my 20's is... _____

_____
_____
_____
_____

A few of my favorite things to cook back then were... _____

_____
_____
_____
_____
_____

Recipe 22 : _____

Serves : _____ **Prep Time :** _____ **Cook Time :** _____

INGREDIENTS :

🌱 _____
🌱 _____
🌱 _____
🌱 _____
🌱 _____
🌱 _____
🌱 _____
🌱 _____
🌱 _____

🌱 _____
🌱 _____
🌱 _____
🌱 _____
🌱 _____
🌱 _____
🌱 _____
🌱 _____
🌱 _____

INSTRUCTIONS :

_____
_____
_____

Hear Your Story Family Keepsake Recipe Journal

Where did you learn this recipe?

THE STORY OF THIS RECIPE

The story of how I learned to cook this recipe is... _____

_____

_____

_____

_____

This is how long it has been in the family... _____

_____

_____

_____

The last time I cooked it was... _____

_____

_____

_____

This is how I would describe how it should taste... _____

_____

_____

_____

And this is the way it makes the house smell when it is cooking... _____

_____

_____

When I think back and remember eating this, these are the memories that come to mind...

_____
_____
_____
_____

MY FOOD STORY IS...

The primary kitchen skills I think every home cook should know are..._____
_____
_____
_____
_____
_____
_____
_____
_____
_____
_____
_____
_____

Recipe 23 : _____

Serves : _____ **Prep Time :** _____ **Cook Time :** _____

INGREDIENTS :

INSTRUCTIONS :

Hear Your Story Family Keepsake Recipe Journal

Where did you learn this recipe?

THE STORY OF THIS RECIPE

The story of how I learned to cook this recipe is... _____
_____
_____
_____
_____

This is how long it has been in the family... _____
_____
_____

The last time I cooked it was... _____
_____
_____

This is how I would describe how it should taste... _____
_____
_____

And this is the way it makes the house smell when it is cooking... _____
_____
_____

When I think back and remember eating this, these are the memories that come to mind...

_____
_____
_____
_____

MY FOOD STORY IS...

A few of my favorite kitchen and cooking shortcuts are... _____
_____
_____
_____
_____
_____

My go-to "company unexpectedly showed up" dish to serve is... _____
_____
_____
_____
_____
_____

Recipe 24 : _____

Serves : _____ **Prep Time :** _____ **Cook Time :** _____

INGREDIENTS :

INSTRUCTIONS :

Hear Your Story Family Keepsake Recipe Journal

Where did you learn this recipe?

THE STORY OF THIS RECIPE

The story of how I learned to cook this recipe is...

This is how long it has been in the family...

The last time I cooked it was...

This is how I would describe how it should taste...

And this is the way it makes the house smell when it is cooking...

When I think back and remember eating this, these are the memories that come to mind...

_____
_____
_____
_____

MY FOOD STORY IS...

My favorite entrée to cook for a crowd is... _____

_____
_____
_____

My favorite dish to cook when I want to impress is... _____

_____
_____
_____

My favorite thing to bring to a potluck is... _____

_____
_____
_____

Recipe 25 : _____

Serves : _____ **Prep Time :** _____ **Cook Time :** _____

INGREDIENTS :

- _____
- _____
- _____
- _____
- _____
- _____
- _____
- _____
- _____

- _____
- _____
- _____
- _____
- _____
- _____
- _____
- _____
- _____

INSTRUCTIONS :

_____

_____

_____

Where did you learn this recipe?

THE STORY OF THIS RECIPE

The story of how I learned to cook this recipe is... _____
_____
_____
_____
_____

This is how long it has been in the family... _____
_____
_____

The last time I cooked it was... _____
_____
_____

This is how I would describe how it should taste... _____
_____
_____

And this is the way it makes the house smell when it is cooking... _____
_____
_____

When I think back and remember eating this, these are the memories that come to mind...

_____
_____
_____
_____

MY FOOD STORY IS...

My favorite ingredient to cook with is... _____

_____
_____
_____

My favorite herb or spice to cook with is... _____

_____
_____
_____

The dish I often make when I just need to get food on the table is... _____

_____
_____
_____
_____

"A FATHER IS SOMEONE YOU LOOK UP TO NO MATTER HOW TALL YOU'VE GROWN."

– AUTHOR UNKNOWN

MY FOOD STORY IS...

The person I most look up to as a cook is... _____
_____
_____

The recipe of theirs that I wish I could make as well as they do is... _____
_____
_____

This is how they have influenced how I cook... _____
_____
_____
_____
_____
_____
_____
_____

Recipe 26 : _____

Serves : _____ **Prep Time :** _____ **Cook Time :** _____

INGREDIENTS :

- _____
- _____
- _____
- _____
- _____
- _____
- _____
- _____
- _____

- _____
- _____
- _____
- _____
- _____
- _____
- _____
- _____
- _____

INSTRUCTIONS :

_____

_____

_____

Where did you learn this recipe?

THE STORY OF THIS RECIPE

The story of how I learned to cook this recipe is... _____
_____
_____
_____
_____

This is how long it has been in the family... _____
_____
_____

The last time I cooked it was... _____
_____
_____

This is how I would describe how it should taste... _____
_____
_____

And this is the way it makes the house smell when it is cooking... _____
_____
_____

When I think back and remember eating this, these are the memories that come to mind…

_____
_____
_____
_____

MY FOOD STORY IS…

A memory of a time when I was especially proud of a meal I prepared and served is… _____
_____
_____
_____
_____
_____

I think the reason this meal stands out in my memories is because… _____
_____
_____
_____
_____
_____

Recipe 27 : _____

Serves : _____ **Prep Time :** _____ **Cook Time :** _____

INGREDIENTS :

INSTRUCTIONS :

Hear Your Story Family Keepsake Recipe Journal

Where did you learn this recipe?

THE STORY OF THIS RECIPE

The story of how I learned to cook this recipe is... _____
_____
_____
_____
_____

This is how long it has been in the family... _____
_____
_____

The last time I cooked it was... _____
_____
_____

This is how I would describe how it should taste... _____
_____
_____

And this is the way it makes the house smell when it is cooking... _____
_____
_____

When I think back and remember eating this, these are the memories that come to mind...

_____
_____
_____
_____

MY FOOD STORY IS...

My favorite kitchen appliance is... _____
_____
_____
_____

My favorite kitchen gadget or tool is... _____
_____
_____
_____

My favorite cookbook is... _____
_____
_____
_____

Recipe 28 : _____

Serves : _____ **Prep Time :** _____ **Cook Time :** _____

INGREDIENTS :

INSTRUCTIONS :

Hear Your Story Family Keepsake Recipe Journal

Where did you learn this recipe?

THE STORY OF THIS RECIPE

The story of how I learned to cook this recipe is... _____
_____
_____
_____
_____

This is how long it has been in the family... _____
_____
_____

The last time I cooked it was... _____
_____
_____

This is how I would describe how it should taste... _____
_____
_____

And this is the way it makes the house smell when it is cooking... _____
_____
_____

When I think back and remember eating this, these are the memories that come to mind...

_____
_____
_____
_____

MY FOOD STORY IS...

My favorite ways to discover new recipes and get ideas for new things to cook are... _____

_____
_____
_____
_____
_____
_____
_____
_____
_____
_____
_____
_____

Recipe 29 : _____

Serves : _____ **Prep Time :** _____ **Cook Time :** _____

INGREDIENTS :

INSTRUCTIONS :

Hear Your Story Family Keepsake Recipe Journal

Where did you learn this recipe?

THE STORY OF THIS RECIPE

The story of how I learned to cook this recipe is... _____
_____
_____
_____
_____

This is how long it has been in the family... _____
_____
_____

The last time I cooked it was... _____
_____
_____

This is how I would describe how it should taste... _____
_____
_____

And this is the way it makes the house smell when it is cooking... _____
_____
_____

When I think back and remember eating this, these are the memories that come to mind…

___

MY FOOD STORY IS…

The story of how I learned this recipe is… ___

This is how long it has been in the family… ___

Recipe 30 : _____

Serves : _____ **Prep Time :** _____ **Cook Time :** _____

INGREDIENTS :

INSTRUCTIONS :

Hear Your Story Family Keepsake Recipe Journal

Where did you learn this recipe?

THE STORY OF THIS RECIPE

The story of how I learned to cook this recipe is... _____
_____
_____
_____
_____

This is how long it has been in the family... _____
_____
_____
_____

The last time I cooked it was... _____
_____
_____
_____

This is how I would describe how it should taste... _____
_____
_____
_____

And this is the way it makes the house smell when it is cooking... _____
_____
_____

When I think back and remember eating this, these are the memories that come to mind...

_____
_____
_____
_____

MY FOOD STORY IS...

The times that I tend to strickly follow a recipe are when cooking... _____

> "THE ONLY TIME TO EAT DIET FOOD IS WHILE YOU'RE WAITING FOR THE STEAK TO COOK."
>
> – JULIA CHILD

MY FOOD STORY IS...

These are the family recipes I hope are still being cooked and enjoyed by our family decades in the future... _____

_____
_____
_____
_____
_____
_____
_____
_____
_____
_____
_____
_____
_____
_____
_____
_____

Recipe 31 : _____

Serves : _____ **Prep Time :** _____ **Cook Time :** _____

INGREDIENTS :

INSTRUCTIONS :

Hear Your Story Family Keepsake Recipe Journal

Where did you learn this recipe?

THE STORY OF THIS RECIPE

The story of how I learned to cook this recipe is... _____

_____

_____

_____

_____

This is how long it has been in the family... _____

_____

_____

The last time I cooked it was... _____

_____

_____

This is how I would describe how it should taste... _____

_____

_____

And this is the way it makes the house smell when it is cooking... _____

_____

_____

When I think back and remember eating this, these are the memories that come to mind...

_____
_____
_____
_____

MY FOOD STORY IS...

The family dish from when I was growing up that I wish I had the recipe for is... _____
_____
_____
_____
_____

Thinking about this dish brings forward these memories... _____
_____
_____
_____
_____
_____

Recipe 32 : _____

Serves : _____ **Prep Time :** _____ **Cook Time :** _____

INGREDIENTS :

INSTRUCTIONS :

Hear Your Story Family Keepsake Recipe Journal

Where did you learn this recipe?

THE STORY OF THIS RECIPE

The story of how I learned to cook this recipe is... _____
_____
_____
_____
_____

This is how long it has been in the family... _____
_____
_____

The last time I cooked it was... _____
_____
_____

This is how I would describe how it should taste... _____
_____
_____

And this is the way it makes the house smell when it is cooking... _____
_____
_____

When I think back and remember eating this, these are the memories that come to mind...

_____
_____
_____
_____

MY FOOD STORY IS...

The recipe I often cook that goes the farthest back in our family's history is... _____
_____
_____
_____

The story and history of this recipe is... _____
_____
_____
_____
_____
_____
_____

Recipe 33 : _____

Serves : _____ **Prep Time :** _____ **Cook Time :** _____

INGREDIENTS :

INSTRUCTIONS :

Hear Your Story Family Keepsake Recipe Journal

Where did you learn this recipe?

THE STORY OF THIS RECIPE

The story of how I learned to cook this recipe is... _____
_____
_____
_____
_____

This is how long it has been in the family... _____
_____
_____

The last time I cooked it was... _____
_____
_____

This is how I would describe how it should taste... _____
_____
_____

And this is the way it makes the house smell when it is cooking... _____
_____
_____

When I think back and remember eating this, these are the memories that come to mind...

_____
_____
_____
_____

MY FOOD STORY IS...

The family dish I would most miss if I could never have it again is... _____
_____
_____
_____
_____
_____

I think the reason this one dish means so much to me is... _____
_____
_____
_____
_____
_____

Recipe 34 : _____

Serves : _____ **Prep Time :** _____ **Cook Time :** _____

INGREDIENTS :

INSTRUCTIONS :

Hear Your Story Family Keepsake Recipe Journal

Where did you learn this recipe?

THE STORY OF THIS RECIPE

The story of how I learned this recipe is... _____

_____

_____

_____

_____

This is how long it has been in the family... _____

_____

_____

The last time I cooked it was... _____

_____

_____

This is how I would describe how it should taste... _____

_____

_____

And this is the way it makes the house smell when it is cooking... _____

_____

_____

When I think back and remember eating this, these are the memories that come to mind...

_____
_____
_____
_____

MY FOOD STORY IS...

When I was growing up, the dish that was often served that I dreaded and did everything to avoid eating was... _____

_____
_____
_____

When I wouldn't eat it, my parents would... _____

_____
_____
_____
_____
_____

Recipe 35 : _____

Serves : _____ **Prep Time :** _____ **Cook Time :** _____

INGREDIENTS :

- _____
- _____
- _____
- _____
- _____
- _____
- _____
- _____
- _____

- _____
- _____
- _____
- _____
- _____
- _____
- _____
- _____
- _____

INSTRUCTIONS :

_____

_____

_____

Hear Your Story Family Keepsake Recipe Journal

Where did you learn this recipe?

THE STORY OF THIS RECIPE

The story of how I learned to cook this recipe is... _____

_____

_____

_____

_____

This is how long it has been in the family... _____

_____

_____

The last time I cooked it was... _____

_____

_____

This is how I would describe how it should taste... _____

_____

_____

And this is the way it makes the house smell when it is cooking... _____

_____

_____

When I think back and remember eating this, these are the memories that come to mind...

_____
_____
_____
_____

MY FOOD STORY IS...

When I think of the foods and dishes we ate and enjoyed when I was growing up, there are several that I now wince at the thought of eating. These include... _____

_____
_____
_____
_____
_____
_____
_____
_____
_____
_____
_____

MY FOOD STORY IS...

If I was to describe what my perfect day would look like as if it were a recipe, it would be...

I would call this recipe... _____

The ingredients of my perfect day would include:

And the directions to make that day happen would be... _____

- _____
- _____
- _____
- _____
- _____
- _____

- _____
- _____
- _____
- _____
- _____
- _____

_____
_____
_____
_____
_____

MY FOOD STORY IS...

One of my most memorable meals that we as a family shared is... _____

_____
_____
_____
_____
_____
_____

One of my most memorable meals that we as a family shared is... _____

_____
_____
_____
_____
_____
_____
_____
_____
_____

Recipe 36 : _____

Serves : _____ **Prep Time :** _____ **Cook Time :** _____

INGREDIENTS :

INSTRUCTIONS :

Hear Your Story Family Keepsake Recipe Journal

Where did you learn this recipe?

THE STORY OF THIS RECIPE

The story of how I learned to cook this recipe is... _____
_____
_____
_____
_____

This is how long it has been in the family... _____
_____
_____

The last time I cooked it was... _____
_____
_____

This is how I would describe how it should taste... _____
_____
_____

And this is the way it makes the house smell when it is cooking... _____
_____
_____

When I think back and remember eating this, these are the memories that come to mind...

___

MY FOOD STORY IS...

If I had to pick between "ate anything" or "picky eater," I would describe how I was as a kid this way... ___

Things I disliked eating when I was a kid but love now include... ___

Recipe 37 : _____

Serves : _____ **Prep Time :** _____ **Cook Time :** _____

INGREDIENTS :

- _____
- _____
- _____
- _____
- _____
- _____
- _____
- _____
- _____

- _____
- _____
- _____
- _____
- _____
- _____
- _____
- _____
- _____

INSTRUCTIONS :

_____
_____
_____

Hear Your Story Family Keepsake Recipe Journal

Where did you learn this recipe?

THE STORY OF THIS RECIPE

The story of how I learned to cook this recipe is… _____
_____
_____
_____
_____

This is how long it has been in the family… _____
_____
_____

The last time I cooked it was… _____
_____
_____

This is how I would describe how it should taste… _____
_____
_____

And this is the way it makes the house smell when it is cooking… _____
_____
_____

When I think back and remember eating this, these are the memories that come to mind…

_____
_____
_____
_____

MY FOOD STORY IS…

When I was a kid, my favorite thing to have for my birthday meal was… _____

_____
_____
_____
_____
_____

And my favorite kind of birthday cake was… _____

_____
_____
_____
_____
_____

Recipe 38 : _____

Serves : _____ **Prep Time :** _____ **Cook Time :** _____

INGREDIENTS :

- _____
- _____
- _____
- _____
- _____
- _____
- _____
- _____
- _____

- _____
- _____
- _____
- _____
- _____
- _____
- _____
- _____
- _____

INSTRUCTIONS :

_____
_____
_____

Hear Your Story Family Keepsake Recipe Journal

Where did you learn this recipe?

THE STORY OF THIS RECIPE

The story of how I learned to cook this recipe is... _____

_____

_____

_____

This is how long it has been in the family... _____

_____

_____

The last time I cooked it was... _____

_____

_____

This is how I would describe how it should taste... _____

_____

_____

And this is the way it makes the house smell when it is cooking... _____

_____

_____

When I think back and remember eating this, these are the memories that come to mind...

_____
_____
_____
_____

MY FOOD STORY IS...

On school days, I typically... _____

◇ Brought my lunch.

◇ Ate the cafeteria food.

◇ Other: _____

When I did bring my lunch to school, it usually consisted of... _____
_____
_____

And this is what I remember about the cafeteria food... _____
_____
_____
_____

Recipe 39 : _____

Serves : _____ **Prep Time :** _____ **Cook Time :** _____

INGREDIENTS :

- _____
- _____
- _____
- _____
- _____
- _____
- _____
- _____
- _____

- _____
- _____
- _____
- _____
- _____
- _____
- _____
- _____
- _____

INSTRUCTIONS :

_____

_____

_____

Hear Your Story Family Keepsake Recipe Journal

Where did you learn this recipe?

THE STORY OF THIS RECIPE

The story of how I learned to cook this recipe is… _____
_____
_____
_____
_____

This is how long it has been in the family… _____
_____
_____

The last time I cooked it was… _____
_____
_____

This is how I would describe how it should taste… _____
_____
_____

And this is the way it makes the house smell when it is cooking… _____
_____
_____

When I think back and remember eating this, these are the memories that come to mind...

_____
_____
_____
_____

MY FOOD STORY IS...

When I was a kid, I would be given the following to eat when I wasn't feeling well... _____

_____
_____
_____
_____
_____

And these are the things I made for my kids when they felt under the weather... _____

_____
_____
_____
_____
_____

Recipe 40 : _____

Serves : _____ **Prep Time :** _____ **Cook Time :** _____

INGREDIENTS :
- _____
- _____
- _____
- _____
- _____
- _____
- _____
- _____
- _____

- _____
- _____
- _____
- _____
- _____
- _____
- _____
- _____
- _____

INSTRUCTIONS :
_____
_____
_____

Hear Your Story Family Keepsake Recipe Journal

Where did you learn this recipe?

THE STORY OF THIS RECIPE

The story of how I learned to cook this recipe is… _____
_____
_____
_____
_____

This is how long it has been in the family… _____
_____
_____

The last time I cooked it was… _____
_____
_____

This is how I would describe how it should taste… _____
_____
_____

And this is the way it makes the house smell when it is cooking… _____
_____
_____

When I think back and remember eating this, these are the memories that come to mind…

_____
_____
_____
_____

MY FOOD STORY IS…

My favorite cuisine to eat is… _____
_____
_____

My favorite cuisine to cook is… _____
_____
_____
_____

The cuisine I would love to learn how to cook is… _____
_____
_____
_____

"EVERYTHING I AM, YOU HELPED ME TO BE."

– AUTHOR UNKNOWN

MY FOOD STORY IS...

Traveling generates opportunities to experience new food and dishes in unforgettable settings, making for lifelong memories. The meals and dishes I most remember while traveling include...

Recipe 41 : _____

Serves : _____ **Prep Time :** _____ **Cook Time :** _____

INGREDIENTS :

- _____
- _____
- _____
- _____
- _____
- _____
- _____
- _____
- _____

- _____
- _____
- _____
- _____
- _____
- _____
- _____
- _____
- _____

INSTRUCTIONS :

_____
_____
_____

Where did you learn this recipe?

THE STORY OF THIS RECIPE

The story of how I learned to cook this recipe is... _____
_____
_____
_____
_____

This is how long it has been in the family... _____
_____
_____

The last time I cooked it was... _____
_____
_____

This is how I would describe how it should taste... _____
_____
_____

And this is the way it makes the house smell when it is cooking... _____
_____
_____

When I think back and remember eating this, these are the memories that come to mind...

_____
_____
_____
_____

MY FOOD STORY IS...

The foods I most associate with a romantic dinner for two are... _____
_____
_____

The foods/dishes I most associate with tailgating or watching sports are... _____
_____
_____
_____

The foods/dishes I most associate with taking a long road trip are... _____
_____
_____
_____

Recipe 42 : _____

Serves : _____ **Prep Time :** _____ **Cook Time :** _____

INGREDIENTS :

INSTRUCTIONS :

Hear Your Story Family Keepsake Recipe Journal

Where did you learn this recipe?

THE STORY OF THIS RECIPE

The story of how I learned to cook this recipe is... _____
_____
_____
_____
_____

This is how long it has been in the family... _____
_____
_____

The last time I cooked it was... _____
_____
_____

This is how I would describe how it should taste... _____
_____
_____

And this is the way it makes the house smell when it is cooking... _____
_____
_____

When I think back and remember eating this, these are the memories that come to mind...

_____
_____
_____
_____

MY FOOD STORY IS...

My favorite comfort foods are... _____
_____
_____
_____
_____
_____

Of these, the ones I most directly associate with my childhood are... _____
_____
_____
_____
_____
_____

Recipe 43: _____

Serves : _____ **Prep Time :** _____ **Cook Time :** _____

INGREDIENTS :

INSTRUCTIONS :

Hear Your Story Family Keepsake Recipe Journal

Where did you learn this recipe?

THE STORY OF THIS RECIPE

The story of how I learned to cook this recipe is... _____
_____
_____
_____
_____

This is how long it has been in the family... _____
_____
_____

The last time I cooked it was... _____
_____
_____

This is how I would describe how it should taste... _____
_____
_____

And this is the way it makes the house smell when it is cooking... _____
_____
_____

When I think back and remember eating this, these are the memories that come to mind...

_____
_____
_____
_____

MY FOOD STORY IS...

My favorite thing to have for breakfast is... _____

_____
_____

The dish that makes me feel healthy and gives me an energy boost is... _____

_____
_____
_____

The food I most enjoy indulging in despite knowing it isn't the best for me is... _____

_____
_____
_____

Recipe 44: _____

Serves : _____ **Prep Time :** _____ **Cook Time :** _____

INGREDIENTS :

- _____
- _____
- _____
- _____
- _____
- _____
- _____
- _____
- _____

- _____
- _____
- _____
- _____
- _____
- _____
- _____
- _____
- _____

INSTRUCTIONS :

_____

_____

_____

Hear Your Story Family Keepsake Recipe Journal

Where did you learn this recipe?

THE STORY OF THIS RECIPE

The story of how I learned to cook this recipe is... _____
_____
_____
_____
_____

This is how long it has been in the family... _____
_____
_____

The last time I cooked it was... _____
_____
_____

This is how I would describe how it should taste... _____
_____
_____

And this is the way it makes the house smell when it is cooking... __
_____
_____

When I think back and remember eating this, these are the memories that come to mind...

_____
_____
_____
_____

MY FOOD STORY IS...

My favorite thing to eat or drink on a rainy day is... _____
_____
_____
_____

The food or drink that refreshes me on a hot day is... _____
_____
_____
_____

The thing I love to eat or drink on a really cold day is... _____
_____
_____
_____

Recipe 45: _____

Serves : _____ **Prep Time :** _____ **Cook Time :** _____

INGREDIENTS :

INSTRUCTIONS :

Hear Your Story Family Keepsake Recipe Journal

Where did you learn this recipe?

THE STORY OF THIS RECIPE

The story of how I learned to cook this recipe is... _____
_____
_____
_____
_____

This is how long it has been in the family... _____
_____
_____

The last time I cooked it was... _____
_____
_____

This is how I would describe how it should taste... _____
_____
_____

And this is the way it makes the house smell when it is cooking... _____
_____
_____

When I think back and remember eating this, these are the memories that come to mind...

___

___

___

___

MY FOOD STORY IS...

Over the years, the principal ways I have modified the way I coook to acccomodate dietary restrictions or preferences are... ___

___

___

___

___

___

___

___

___

___

___

"FOR ME, COOKING IS AN EXTENSION OF LOVE."

– HEDDA STERNE

MY FOOD STORY IS...

When I think back to all of the meals I have experienced during my life, the one that I think has to be my favorite is... _____

_____

_____

_____

This is what I remember about this meal... _____

_____

_____

_____

_____

_____

_____

_____

_____

_____

Recipe 46: _____

Serves : _____ **Prep Time :** _____ **Cook Time :** _____

INGREDIENTS :

INSTRUCTIONS :

Where did you learn this recipe?

THE STORY OF THIS RECIPE

The story of how I learned to cook this recipe is... _____
_____
_____
_____
_____

This is how long it has been in the family... _____
_____
_____

The last time I cooked it was... _____
_____
_____

This is how I would describe how it should taste... _____
_____
_____

And this is the way it makes the house smell when it is cooking... _____
_____
_____

When I think back and remember eating this, these are the memories that come to mind…

_____
_____
_____
_____

MY FOOD STORY IS… STILL BEING WRITTEN…

The place I want to travel to so I can experience the food is… _____

_____
_____
_____
_____

The things I find so interesting and appealing about this destination and its cuisine are… _____

_____
_____
_____
_____
_____

Recipe 47: _____

Serves : _____ **Prep Time :** _____ **Cook Time :** _____

INGREDIENTS :

INSTRUCTIONS :

Hear Your Story Family Keepsake Recipe Journal

Where did you learn this recipe?

THE STORY OF THIS RECIPE

The story of how I learned to cook this recipe is... _____
_____
_____
_____
_____

This is how long it has been in the family... _____
_____
_____

The last time I cooked it was... _____
_____
_____

This is how I would describe how it should taste... _____
_____
_____

And this is the way it makes the house smell when it is cooking... _____
_____
_____

When I think back and remember eating this, these are the memories that come to mind...

_____
_____
_____
_____

MY FOOD STORY IS... STILL BEING WRITTEN...

When I think back to when I was just beginning to cook and compare it to where I am now, this is how I would describe how my abilities, confidence, and skills have changed and grown... _____

Recipe 48: _____

Serves : _____ **Prep Time :** _____ **Cook Time :** _____

INGREDIENTS :

INSTRUCTIONS :

Hear Your Story Family Keepsake Recipe Journal

Where did you learn this recipe?

THE STORY OF THIS RECIPE

The story of how I learned to cook this recipe is... _____

_____

_____

_____

_____

This is how long it has been in the family... _____

_____

_____

The last time I cooked it was... _____

_____

_____

This is how I would describe how it should taste... _____

_____

_____

And this is the way it makes the house smell when it is cooking... _____

_____

_____

When I think back and remember eating this, these are the memories that come to mind...

___

MY FOOD STORY IS... STILL BEING WRITTEN...

The things I still want to learn about cooking and food are... ___

Recipe 49: _____

Serves: _____ **Prep Time:** _____ **Cook Time:** _____

INGREDIENTS:

INSTRUCTIONS:

Hear Your Story Family Keepsake Recipe Journal

Where did you learn this recipe?

THE STORY OF THIS RECIPE

The story of how I learned to cook this recipe is... _____
_____
_____
_____
_____

This is how long it has been in the family... _____
_____
_____

The last time I cooked it was... _____
_____
_____

This is how I would describe how it should taste... _____
_____
_____

And this is the way it makes the house smell when it is cooking... _____
_____
_____

When I think back and remember eating this, these are the memories that come to mind...

___

MY FOOD STORY IS... STILL BEING WRITTEN...

If I could cook with and learn from any one person who has ever lived, I would pick... ___

Recipe 50: _____

Serves : _____ **Prep Time :** _____ **Cook Time :** _____

INGREDIENTS :

INSTRUCTIONS :

Hear Your Story Family Keepsake Recipe Journal

Where did you learn this recipe?

THE STORY OF THIS RECIPE

The story of how I learned to cook this recipe is... _____

_____

_____

_____

_____

This is how long it has been in the family... _____

_____

_____

The last time I cooked it was... _____

_____

_____

This is how I would describe how it should taste... _____

_____

_____

And this is the way it makes the house smell when it is cooking... _____

_____

_____

When I think back and remember eating this, these are the memories that come to mind…

_____
_____
_____
_____

MY FOOD STORY IS… STILL BEING WRITTEN…

When I think back to my food mentors and teachers, I think they would be proud of the cook I have become because… _____

_____
_____
_____
_____
_____
_____
_____
_____
_____
_____

MY FOOD STORY IS... STILL BEING WRITTEN...

When I reflect on all the meals I have prepared and all the people I have fed, I am grateful for and proud of myself for all of the following... _____

_____
_____
_____
_____
_____
_____
_____
_____
_____
_____
_____
_____
_____
_____
_____
_____
_____

"LIFE IS UNCERTAIN. EAT DESSERT FIRST."

— ERNESTINE ULMER

MEASUREMENTS & CONVERSIONS

Measurements	US Standard	Metric
1/8 teaspoon (tsp.)		0.5 milliliter (ml.)
1/4 tsp.		1 ml.
1/2 tsp.		2 ml.
1 tsp.		5 ml.
1 tablespoon (tbsp.)		15 ml.
2 tbsp.	1 fluid ounce (fl. oz.)	30 ml.
1/4 cup	2 fl. oz.	60 ml.
1/3 cup	3 fl. oz.	80 ml.
1/2 cup	4 fl. oz.	120 ml.
2/3 cup	5 fl. oz.	160 ml.
3/4 cup	6 fl. oz.	180 ml.
1 cup	8 fl. oz.	240 ml.
2 cups	16 fl. oz. or 1 pint (pt.)	480 ml.
1 quart (qt.)	64 fl. oz. or 2 pt.	.95 liter (l)

MEASUREMENTS & CONVERSIONS

× × × × ×

Measurements	US Standard	Metric
1 tablespoon (tbsp.)	1/2 fluid ounce (fl. oz.) 3 teaspoons (tsp.)	15 milliliters (ml.)
1/4 cup	2 fl. oz. 12 tsp. 4 tablespoons (tbsp.) 6 fl. oz.	60 ml.
1/3 cup	3 fl. oz. 5 tbsp. + 1 tsp.	80 ml.
1/2 cup	4 fl. oz. 8 tbsp.	120 ml.
3/4 cup	6 fl. oz. 12 tbsp.	180 ml.
1 cup	8 fl. oz. 16 tbsp.	240 ml.
1 pint (pt.)	16 fl. oz. 2 cups	480 ml.
1 quart (qt.)	32 fl. oz. 4 cups 2 pt.	0.95 liter (L)
1 gallon (gal.)	128 fl. oz. 16 cups 8 pt. 4 qt.	120 ml.

Hear Your Story
Books & Guided Journals

At Hear Your Story, we have created a line of books focused on giving each of us a place to tell the unique story of who we are, where we have been, and where we are going.

Sharing and hearing the stories of the people in our life creates a closeness and understanding, ultimately strengthening our bonds.

Mom, I Want to Hear Your Story:
A Mother's Guided Journal to Share Her Life & Her Love

Dad, I Want to Hear Your Story:
A Father's Guided Journal to Share His Life & His Love

Grandmother, I Want to Hear Your Story:
A Grandmother's Guided Journal to Share Her Life and Her Love

Grandfather, I Want to Hear Your Story:
A Grandmother's Guided Journal to Share His Life and His Love

Tell Your Life Story: The Write Your Own Autobiography Guided Journal

To My Wonderful Aunt, I Want to Hear Your Story:

A Guided Journal to Share Her Life and Her Love

To My Uncle, I Want to Hear Your Story:

A Guided Journal to Share His Life and His Love

Mom, I Want to Learn Your Recipes:

A Keepsake Memory Journal to Gather & Preserve Your Favorite Family Recipes

Grandmother, I Want to Learn Your Recipes:

A Keepsake Memory Journal to Gather & Preserve Your Favorite Family Recipes

Aunt, I Want to Learn Your Recipes:

A Keepsake Memory Journal to Gather & Preserve Your Favorite Family Recipes

Mom & Me: Let's Learn Together Journal for Kids

FIND MORE FAMILY CONNECTION AT

hearyourstorybooks   www.hearyourstorybooks.com

ABOUT THE AUTHOR

Jeffrey Mason is the creator and author of the best-selling Hear Your Story® line of books and is the founder of the company Hear Your Story®.

In response to his own father's fight with Alzheimer's, Jeffrey wrote his first two books, Mom, I Want to Hear Your Story and Dad, I Want to Hear Your Story in 2018. Since then, he has written and designed over 30 books, been published in four languages, and sold over 300,000 copies worldwide.

Jeffrey is dedicated to spreading the mission that the little things are the big things and that each of us has an incredible life story that needs to be shared and celebrated. He continues to create books that he hopes will guide people to reflect on and share their full life experience, while creating opportunities for talking, listening, learning, and understanding.

Hear Your Story can be visited at hearyourstorybooks.com and Jeffrey can be contacted for questions, comments, podcasting, speaking engagements, or just a hello at jeffrey.mason@hearyourstory.com.

He would be grateful if you would help people find his books by leaving a review on Amazon. Your feedback helps him get better at this thing he loves.

Copyright © 2023 EYP Publishing, LLC,
Hear Your Story® Books, & Jeff ey Mason
All rights reserved. No part of this publication may be reproduced, distributed,
or transmitted in any form or by any means, including photocopying, recording, computer,
or other electronic or mechanical methods, without the prior written permission of the publisher,
except in the case of brief quotations embodied in critical reviews and certain other noncommercial uses
permitted by copyright law. For permission requests, write to the publisher, addressed
"Attention: Permissions Coordinator," to customerservice@eyppublishing.com.
ISBN: 978-1-955034-79-1

Made in the USA
Middletown, DE
23 January 2024